Alice Ramsey's
Grand Adventure

Written and Illustrated by Don Brown

Houghton Mifflin Company Boston 1997

For information about this and other Houghton Mifflin trade and
reference books and multimedia products, visit The Bookstore at Houghton Mifflin
on the World Wide Web at http://www.hmco.com/trade/.

The text of this book is set in 14 point Palatino.
The illustrations are watercolor, reproduced in full color.

Library of Congress Cataloging-in-Publication Data

Brown, Don.
Alice Ramsey's grand adventure / by Don Brown.
p.   cm.
Summary: Describes the difficulties faced by the first woman to make a
cross-country journey from New York to San Francisco in an automobile in 1909.
ISBN 0-395-70127-9
1. United States—Description and travel—Juvenile literature.   2. Automobile travel—United
States—History—20th century—Juvenile literature.   3. Ramsey, Alice—Juvenile literature.
4. Women travelers—United States—History—20th century—Juvenile literature.
[1. Ramsey, Alice. 2. Automobile travel. 3. Women—Biography.] I. Title.
E168.B8836   1997
917.304'911—dc20   96-31783   CIP   AC

Manufactured in the United States of America
HOR 10 9 8 7 6 5 4 3 2 1

For Deborah, who knows great hope is better than good sense.

On June 9, 1909, Alice Ramsey drove out of New York City and into a grand adventure. Alice Ramsey wanted to be the first woman to drive across America.

Alice's friend, Hermine, and her sisters-in-law, Nettie and Margaret, traveled with her. They knew nothing about automobiles. The car's good repair would be Alice's job, although the Maxwell company—the maker of the touring car and the sponsor of the trip—promised to help.

The Maxwell needed keen attention. Alice used a stick to measure the gasoline in the twenty-gallon tank under the front seat. The headlamps were torches enclosed in brass housings and Alice had to light them with a match! The horn was a rubber bulb.

While Alice steered the car, adjusted the levers, and attended the engine, she also had to find her way. The few roads were narrow and dusty, more accustomed to horses' hooves than automobile tires. There were no road signs. She would have to ask directions or follow instructions from the Blue Book.

The Blue Book was the only guidebook for motorists, and it covered just the eastern United States. It told the miles between towns and the turns to make. Turn left at the red barn with the yellow silo, it might say. Excellent directions as long as the farmer hadn't repainted the silo blue.

America slowly revealed itself: New York State, Pennsylvania, Ohio, Indiana. Towns and cities came and went. They passed many, many farms.

Near Toledo, Ohio,
Alice raced the Maxwell
at top speed—forty-two miles an hour!

It was slower going over a road in Illinois.
The way was clogged with pigs—
big pigs, little pigs,
brown, black, and pink pigs!

Chicago, Illinois, was a railroad center. The car bounced over mile after mile of rail until the women were dizzy.

Just west of the Mississippi River, the rain started. It rained and rained. The dirt road dissolved into a thick, filthy stew. It was nearly impossible to drive.

After plowing many miles through the choking mud, they reached a stream called Weasel Creek. It had overflowed its banks and submerged the small bridge over it.

Alice removed her boots and skirt. She stepped from the car and held her long slip pulled to the front. Using an umbrella to steady herself, she gingerly waded into the stream to measure its depth.

It was too deep for the Maxwell to cross!

The women waited for the river to recede, picnicking on bread and water bought for twenty-five cents at a nearby farm. Darkness came. They hung the side panels to the Maxwell's top. Alice rested her feet on the dashboard. The others found their own rough comfort as they tried to sleep.

By dawn the next day, the stream was low enough for Alice to drive the Maxwell across. But the rain and mud made progress nearly impossible.

"Ship the Maxwell by rail past the difficulties," local residents urged Alice.

"I'll drive every inch of the way if it kills me!" Alice replied.

To lighten the car, it was decided that Hermine, Nettie, and Margaret would travel by train to be met later by Alice. But Alice wouldn't be traveling alone. J.D. Murphy, a man who worked for the Maxwell Company, would ride along with her.

Alice set off across Nebraska with her new passenger. Craters filled with water pocked the road. Alice drove carefully. The Maxwell lurched, plopped, and skidded. Suddenly the Maxwell's front and rear tires plunged into separate holes! They were stuck!

How could they escape?

J.D. trudged to the back of the Maxwell and wedged a piece of wood under the rear tire. Alice edged the car forward as J.D. pushed. The Maxwell strained mightily and then hopped out of its trap, splattering J.D. with mud!

Alice and J.D. continued west.

Hermine, Nettie, and Margaret eventually rejoined Alice in Sioux City, South Dakota. The rain ended but travel remained hard.

The car dropped into a huge pothole. A boy driving a team of horses dragged it out.

The Maxwell's brake pedal broke. Alice slid
beneath the car and fixed it with a snip of wire.

The Maxwell's axle snapped and Alice
and another mechanic installed a replacement.

A hail storm erupted, and the women sought shelter
at a nearby farm owned by a family that spoke only Danish.

In Wyoming, the road climbed gravelly hills, known as arroyos. The struggling Maxwell kept sliding backward. Alice had Margaret, Nettie, and Hermine stand alongside the car and slip blocks of wood behind the tires. They repeated this inch by inch until they reached the crest.

The Platte River was the next hurdle. The only span over it was a railroad bridge. Alice eased the Maxwell over the crossing. She drove carefully and kept moving—if she didn't, the Maxwell's tires would become trapped between the railroad ties. *Bump! Bump! Bump!* There were nearly a mile of *Bumps!* before they reached the other side.

The road was just a wagon trail and sometimes disappeared altogether. Alice followed telephone lines, hoping the wires would lead her to the next town. It wasn't always successful—sometimes it left them even more lost.

Alice and her friends reached Utah. Miles of desert stretched before them. It was wild land and Alice wanted to cross it quickly.

Long, hot days of driving passed, sometimes starting before dawn and lasting hours into the night. Once, Alice drove seventeen hours, napped for three hours on a bed made from the Maxwell's seat cushions, then continued driving.

The sandy path carried the pioneers into Nevada. Horned toads and magpies watched the Maxwell skitter by.

The Sierra Nevada Mountains towered before them: Alice's last great obstacle. She steered the Maxwell up the steep path. The road snaked back and forth up the mountain. The car struggled on the incline and its engine became hot. Alice lifted the hood to cool the motor and rested the Maxwell at each turn. It took eight hours to travel seventy miles.

After the grueling climb, the women were thrilled to be in California and near their goal! They crested the Sierra Nevadas and followed the road to Oakland.

Alice guided the Maxwell onto a ferry that carried them to San Francisco.

When she rolled off the ferry behind the wheel of her Maxwell, Alice Ramsey became the first woman to have driven across America!

It was August 7, 1909. Fifty-nine days had passed since Alice left New York City.

A parade of cars escorted them through the city. Horns honked wildly. Spectators cheered and waved. A grand party celebrated Alice Ramsey's feat.

Alice was anxious to return to her home near New York City. But she still thought of new journeys. Over the next seventy years, Alice Ramsey drove across America more than thirty times.